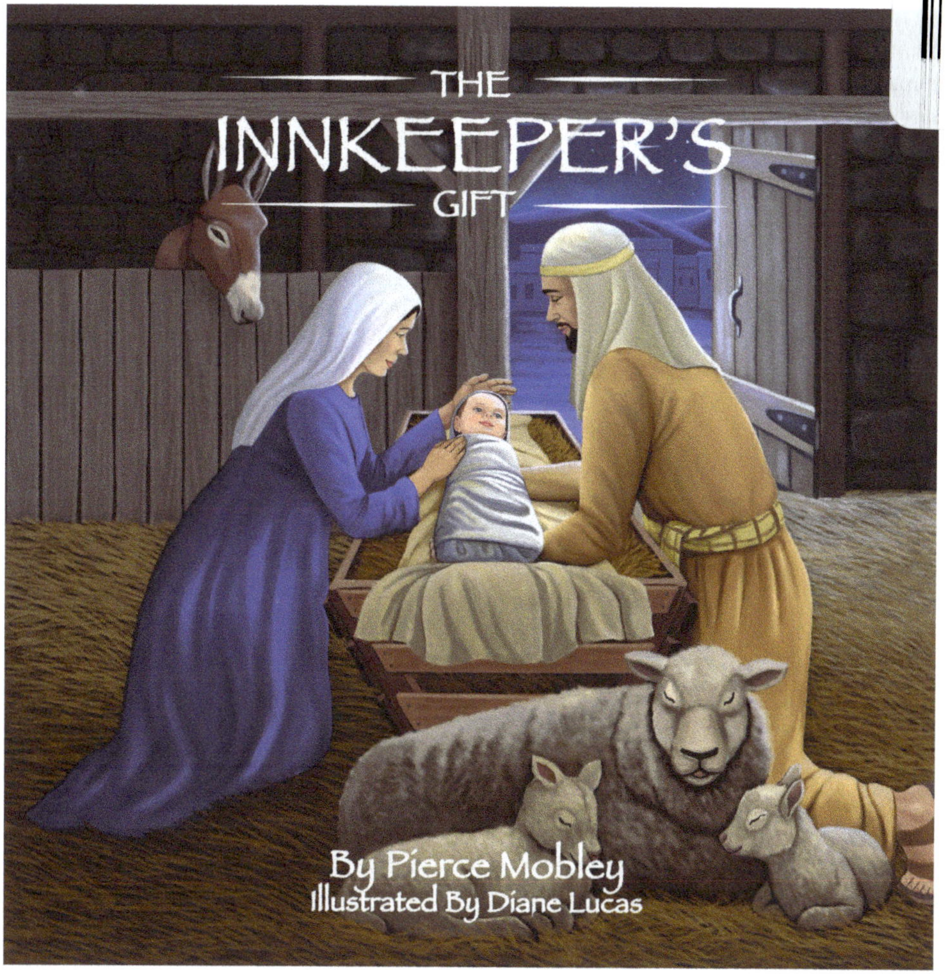

Halo
Publishing International

Please visit us at: www.highwaychaplain.org

Copyright © 2015 Pierce Mobley
Illustrated by Diane Lucas
All rights reserved.

No part of this book may be reproduced in any manner without the written consent of the publisher except for brief excerpts in critical reviews or articles.

ISBN 13: 978-1-61244-347-8
Library of Congress Control Number: 2015904673

Printed in the United States of America

Published by Halo Publishing International
1100 NW Loop 410
Suite 700 - 176
San Antonio, Texas 78213
Toll Free 1-877-705-9647
www.halopublishing.com
www.holapublishing.com
e-mail: contact@halopublishing.com

I WANT TO DEDICATE THIS BOOK TO MY GRANDCHILDREN:
ROBYN, DAMIAN, DUSTIN, ALEXIS, TIMOTHY, TREVOR,
IAN, CHARLEE GRACE, AND AVA.

ALWAYS REMEMBER THAT NO MATTER HOW GREAT OR HOW SMALL
THE GIFT. WHEN YOU PRESENT IT TO GOD TO USE.
IT WILL ALWAYS HAVE ETERNAL BENEFIT.

SO REMEMBER THAT THE LORD HAS GIVEN EACH OF YOU BOTH
TALENTS AND GIFTS BOTH- GREAT AND SMALL,
USE THEM ALWAYS TO GLORIFY GOD.

*Ecclesiastes 11:1 Cast thy bread upon the waters;
for thou shall find it after many days. (KJV)*

A census the words echoed in young Joseph's mind as he worked. How could he even think of traveling to Bethlehem with Mary so close to delivering her first child? The trip would be hard on her and might even harm the unborn babe.

Shaking his head he tried to think of a way to avoid taking such a long trip now.

Maybe I can appeal to the Governor and get permission to delay going to Bethlehem until after the baby is born. Joseph thought, *I'll talk with father. He'll know what to do.*

Finishing his work in the shop Joseph headed home to tell Mary about the news. He passed a Roman soldier posting a notice about the census at the city gates. Many of Nazareth's men complained angrily.

Returning to the city of their ancestors would be hard on everyone. For some it would require closing their businesses and taking large families on a long journey of 100 miles or more. Some would not only have to return to the city of their ancestors, but also to their wives' ancestors' cities to register them. All so the Roman Emperor could tax them and their families more. It frustrated so many of them.

It didn't seem right to disrupt their lives just to make them pay a tax. Why not send out tax collectors to each town and village to collect the tax and count the people? Then people could continue with their lives without all this confusion. It seemed so meaningless.

When Joseph entered the house he shared with his young bride Mary the smell of fresh bread filled the air. Smiling, he washed up and called for Mary. Coming into the room, her face brightened with a smile for Joseph. Always glad to see him she asked about his day.

The look of joy faded from his face as he remembered the notice posted at the town gate. Joseph frowned and said, "There is a census being taken by the Roman Emperor. We will have to go to Bethlehem soon because we must go to the city of our fathers." He took her hands in his.

"I don't want to go, Mary. With you so close to giving birth. I am afraid the trip will be too hard for you and the child. I am going to try to get permission to delay the trip at least until the baby is born."

"But Joseph, must we both go or is it just for you?" Mary asked.

"No, we both must present ourselves to the Roman tax collector to be counted in the census."

Mary squeezed his hands. "No matter I know that God will take care of us. Come, let's eat. I know you must be hungry after such a long day of work."

Joseph tried every way he knew to make different arrangements for himself and Mary. Yet no matter what he tried, the answer was no. It was with great agony that he began to plan the journey to Bethlehem. The time neared when he and Mary would have to leave on their trip.

"I am going to have to sell everything we have to make this trip. You can't walk the seventy miles to Bethlehem and I have no donkey for you to ride Mary. The only things we won't sell are our clothes and my tools. At least I will be able to work and make a little money during the journey," said Joseph.

"What will we do when we return from Bethlehem if we have no place to live?" Mary asked.

"I don't think we will return here for some time after we leave. You will probably give birth while we are in Bethlehem, and I will not take you or the child on another hard journey until you are both strong."

Joseph sold furniture and possessions until he had enough money for the journey and the taxes. With the money, he purchased a donkey. Taking the donkey's halter in his hand, he led him home. Joseph went inside and told Mary of the donkey he had for her to ride.

Mary, by this time, had become great with child. Hearing Joseph had brought the donkey home, she breathed a sigh of relief. Grateful not to have to walk the seventy miles to Bethlehem. The roads were rough and rocky going over large hills. Without something to ride, she knew she would not be able to endure the trip. Even on the back of a donkey, the trip would not be easy.

A few days later Joseph strapped on the saddle and packed up the little donkey. Then, with great care, he hoisted Mary up onto the back of the animal and taking the reins in his hands began the long trip to Bethlehem.

The trip would take them three days to complete and possibly 4 in Mary's condition. They would need to take many rest stops along the way so Mary could stretch her back, and get some relief from the gentle bouncing on the donkey's back.

The dirt on the roads was packed hard. Clearly, the route had been well traveled by all types of people. Everyone from nomadic tribesmen to Roman soldiers to merchants running from one market to another had trodden this soil. A great number of travelers crowded the road, some going in the same direction as Mary and Joseph and many more going the opposite direction. It seemed like all of Israel was on the move.

For 3 long days Joseph and Mary traveled the road leading to Bethlehem. Joseph felt like his feet were made of stone; they seemed so heavy. The sun was beginning to set when he topped a hill and saw Bethlehem in the distance. Just a few more miles to go, and then he and Mary could rest.

They needed to find an inn. It would be pleasant to wash the dirt from the day's journey from their faces, hands and feet. After that they would get a hot meal and cool water to drink. The thought of no more walking caused Joseph to hasten his step. *Just 2 more hills and we will be in the city,* he thought.

A couple of hours later, as the sun's light faded into darkness Joseph and Mary entered the city. Never had Joseph seen such a sight. The streets were flooded with people. It looked like a rolling river of humanity flowing along Bethlehem's narrow streets. Being jostled and pushed by the crowd, Joseph tightened his grip on the reins of the donkey's harness.

Looking up at Mary to reassure her that everything was alright, his stomach tightened with fear. Mary had her head bowed, and she was taking short quick breaths. Sweat beaded her brow and her face was creased as if she were in pain. She saw Joseph looking at her with fear in his face. "It's time!" she gasped

Joseph spotted an inn nearby. With determination he pushed against the crowd towards the door. He banged on the door.

An indignant, aged man opened the door. "What do you want?"

Joseph pointed to Mary, "My wife is in labor." The man's face was unmoved. "Wait, I have money. Please sir, may we stay the night?"

Shaking his head, the innkeeper replied, "Son if I had even the smallest corner, I would not hesitate to let you stay. But I have but a small place at the hearth in which to roll out a mat for myself to sleep. I am sorry, but I am beyond full." He began to shut the door.

Joseph placed his foot in the threshold of the door. "Please sir, I beg you. Is there another inn which might have a little room for us?"

"There is another inn on the opposite side of town. You might check there, but I am afraid you will find he is just as full as I am. I have never seen so many people in all of my life. I hope you find a place to have your child. I am sorry there is no room in my inn."

Frustrated, Joseph turned and started down the street. Pulling the donkey's reins, he pushed his way through the crowds. Looking up and down the streets of Bethlehem for the inn, Joseph heard Mary give a short cry of pain from atop the donkey. Alarmed Joseph searched frantically for the inn. He was tired, but intent on finding a place.

Finally, he saw the inn. With Mary groaning in pain every few minutes, Joseph knew there wasn't much time before the child would be born.

Joseph stepped up to the door and pounded with a fury. His thoughts ran wild with fear every time he heard Mary cry out in pain. "Please, open the door, please." He prayed someone would answer.

With a sigh of relief, he heard the bolt slide and the door creaked open. As he peered into the doorway he saw an elderly man. Gray haired, with a beard hanging from his dry creased face, the innkeeper looked at Joseph and Mary knowing what the young man was about to ask. He held up his hand as if stopping someone from coming closer.

Even before Joseph could ask, the man spoke, "I am sorry young man, but I am filled beyond capacity. There is no room here, go down to the other side of town there is an inn there. Maybe they will have room."

Joseph's voice trembled as he pleaded with the man. "But sir, my wife, is in labor and I fear it will not be long before she gives birth to the child. Please reconsider. I beg of you. We need a place, and the inn across town sent us here for they also are full. Can't you help us, please?"

"I am sorry young man, but I cannot turn out people who have paid for the night. I really have nowhere for your wife to have her child. There are many people here and that is something that should be done privately."

"Please sir we will take any place you have. We would even stay upon the roof if you would let us. We have nowhere else to go and no one to turn to. You are our last hope," Joseph said with tears streaming down his face.

The old man looked at Joseph and shook his head as he began closing the door. "I even have people on the roof. I am filled to overflowing. I am very sorry, but there just isn't any room here."

When the door closed, Joseph leaned his head against it. All of his strength seemed to drain from him. He thought there wasn't any more hope to find a place for the night. He knocked again. Sinking to his knees, he pleaded, "Please sir, have mercy on us I beg you. Please don't leave us out here. My wife is not some stray animal that she should bear her child in the street. If you have anywhere we can stay even just for tonight, I beg you please, please reconsider."

The old innkeeper leaned back against the door listening to Joseph's pleas. He searched his mind and heart trying to figure out where the young couple could stay. Even the homes of his family who lived in other parts of town were filled. The town was overflowing with people and there just wasn't anywhere for this couple to stay.

When he heard Joseph say *stray animal,* the innkeeper bolted upright. *"The stable! They can stay in the stable."* He threw the door open so quickly that Joseph, who had leaned against the door in despair, tumbled in.

Frantically the innkeeper spoke, "My stable, you can stay in the stable if you want. What do you say, son? It's all I have to offer and I won't even charge you for it. That will be my gift to your newborn babe. Will that be sufficient?"

Joseph looked at the innkeeper surprised and speechless for a moment. "Yes, we will take it. But we must hurry, for I fear my wife is near the time of the birth."

They rushed out to the stable. The innkeeper and Joseph put down fresh straw and laid out blankets for Mary to lie down on. They cleaned out the manger to make a crib for the child when it came.

So it was that the Savior of the world, Jesus Christ, was born in the stable of an inn. The innkeeper's gift didn't seem like much at the time. Yet at Christmas each year, the picture of the Savior's birth is framed by "The Innkeeper's Gift."

www.ingramcontent.com/pod-product-compliance
Lightning Source LLC
Chambersburg PA
CBHW041439040426
42453CB00021B/2469